30 Days Vegeta
Healthy Dinne

Eat your way through these nutrient-rich **vegetarian recipes for dinner; to improve heart condition for a whole month and beyond**

Contents

Introduction

Consuming more vegetarian meals is a terrific way to improve your heart health because you eat more fiber and less saturated fat! To fulfill our strict heart-healthy criteria, we adapted these recipes to be incredibly tasty due to a variety of herbs and spices) with only a pinch of salt. For some ideas this month, explore our Grilled Eggplant Tomato Pasta or Chickpea Potato Curry.

My Heart-Friendly Vegetarian Staples of All Time

The key to preparing healthful, substantial vegetarian meals on a weekly basis is to stock up on the right ingredients at the supermarket. If my pantry and refrigerator are stocked with my favorite ingredients, I know I can quickly prepare a great dinner rich in protein, vegetables, and whole grains.

Here are ten vegetarian essentials that are always in my shopping basket.

- **Lentils**

I always buy dry lentils rather than canned because they cook in about 20 minutes and don't require soaking. I have French green lentils in my cupboard for soups and salads (they hold their value nicely) and red lentils in my pantry for curries.

- **Brown Rice & Quinoa**

Since we go through quinoa so rapidly at home, I always reach for a bag (white or red!). I can have a complete protein to add into salads, chilis, and frittatas in 15 minutes. I also grab a bag of short-grain brown rice to stuff inside peppers, use as a basis for black bean burrito bowls, or create kimchi fried rice (I sub lentils for the ground beef here).

- **Avocados**

Avocados find their way into my shopping cart on a regular basis. Topping scrambled egg tacos with guacamole, adding avocado slices to grain bowls, and blitzing an avocado to make my favorite pasta sauce (trust me on this one).

- **Canned Beans**

Despite the fact that I make my own lentils, I frequently use canned beans to supplement my stockpile. I'll open a can of chickpeas to make crispy chickpeas to serve with salads or soups, a can of black beans to create 10-minute tacos, or a can of white beans to make a beans with greens hash.

- **Canned Tomatoes**

My shopping basket is always stocked with entire peeled canned tomatoes. While I enjoy using fresh tomatoes, they are only available for a limited time. When I need to create Marcella Hazan's famed tomato soup, canned tomatoes, on the other hand, are always there for me.

- **Tahini**

Tahini, like avocado, is that magical ingredient that improves any vegetarian meal. I'll use it to top a grain bowl with a turmeric tahini sauce, create a batch of hummus to spread over sandwiches, or make a simple dressing to season green salads.

Eggs While I understand that not all vegetarians consume eggs, they are essential ingredients for my diet. Eggs appear in so many dinners each week, from scrambled egg tacos to a fried egg atop kimchi fried rice to a beautiful soft-boiled egg in a bowl of vegetable ramen.

- **Canned Coconut Milk**

We consume a lot of curries, soups, and peanut sauce, so canned coconut milk is a must-have in our family. When I want to add additional flavor and body to brown rice, I'll cook it in coconut milk. Coconut milk is also used in my breakfast chia pudding and smoothies.

30 Days of Vegetarian Heart-Healthy Dinners

Day 1

<u>Chickpea & Potato Curry</u>

This quick Indian-style curry is made with ingredients you most likely already have on hand, such as frozen peas, canned tomatoes, and chickpeas. Furthermore, the use of these spices demonstrates how simple it is to produce a curry sauce for an easy vegetarian cuisine. To soak it all up, serve with whole-wheat naan.

Recipe Summary

| Active: 35 minutes | Total: 35 minutes | Servings: 4 |

Nutrition Profile:

Heart Healthy	Vegetarian	Low Added
Low-Calorie	Vegan	Sugars
High Fiber	Low Sodium	
Diabetes	High Blood	
Appropriate	Pressure	

Ingredients

- 1 pound Yukon Gold potatoes, peeled and cut into 1-inch pieces
- 3 tablespoons grape seed oil or canola oil
- 1 large onion, diced
- 3 cloves garlic, minced
- ½ teaspoon garam masala
- 2 teaspoons curry powder
- ¾ teaspoon salt
- ¼ teaspoon cayenne pepper
- 1 cup frozen peas
- 1 (14 ounce) can no-salt-added diced tomatoes
- ¾ cup water, divided
- 1 (15 ounce) can low-sodium chickpeas, rinsed

Instructions

• • •

Step 1

Bring 1 inch of water to a boil in a big pot installed with a steamer basket. Put potatoes, cover and steam until tender, 5 to 6 minutes. Set aside the potatoes. Clean the pot.

Step 2

Heat the oil in the pot over medium-high heat. Insert onion, and boil stirring often, until soft and translucent, 2 - 3 minutes. Cook for 1 minute, stirring constantly, after adding the garlic, curry powder, salt, and cayenne. Pour in tomatoes and their juice; cook for 2 minutes Fill a blender or food processor halfway with the mixture. Puree with ½ cup water until smooth.

Step 3

Transfer the puree to the pot. Rinse the sauce residue with the remaining ¼ cup water in the blender or food processor. Add the saved potatoes, chickpeas, peas, and garam masala to the pot. Cook, stirring frequently, for about 5 minutes, or until heated.

Tips

Garam masala, a spice blend consisting of coriander, black pepper, cumin, cardamom, cinnamon, and other spices, provides a warming, nuanced depth of flavor to this Indian stew.

Nutritional Info

Per Serving:

301 Calories; Protein 8g; Carbohydrates 45g; Dietary Fiber 8.8g; Sugars 6g; Fat 16g; Saturated Fat 1.1g; Vitamin A In 968.5IU; Vitamin C 29mg; Folate 32mcg; Calcium 76mg; Iron 4mg; Magnesium 62mg; Potassium 795.6mg; Sodium 538mg

Day 2

Buttermilk Fried Tofu with Smoky Collard Greens

Dip tofu in buttermilk to make the coating stick for crispy pan-fried tofu that tastes like fried chicken. The paprika adds a smoky taste to the collards while making the dish vegetarian. This quick, easy, and healthful supper comes together in only 25 minutes, making it ideal for hectic weeknights.

Recipe Summary

Active: 25 minutes   Total: 25 minutes   Servings: 4

Nutrition Profile:

Heart Healthy	Vegetarian	Healthy Aging
Low-Calorie	Low Sodium	Healthy
Diabetes	Nut-Free	Immunity
Appropriate	High Calcium	Low Added
Egg Free	Bone Health	Sugars

Ingredients

- 6 tablespoons grape seed oil or canola oil, divided

• • •

- 1 (1 pound) package chopped collards
- ½ cup water
- ¾ teaspoon salt, divided
- 1 tablespoon cider vinegar
- ½ teaspoon smoked paprika
- 1 (14 to 16 ounce) package extra-firm tofu, drained
- 1 cup whole-wheat panko
- 1 cup buttermilk
- ½ teaspoon garlic powder
- ½ teaspoon onion powder
- ¼ teaspoon cayenne pepper
- Hot (spicy) honey for serving

Instructions

Step 1

Cook 1 tablespoon oil in a large pot over medium heat. Insert collards and water; cover and cook, stirring occasionally, until soft and crumbled, about 8 minutes. Take the pan off the heat and mix in the vinegar, paprika, and ½ teaspoon salt. Cover to keep it warm.

Step 2

Meanwhile, chop the tofu into 8 equal pieces crosswise. To remove excess water, blot with paper towels. In a 7-by-11-inch baking dish, combine buttermilk, garlic powder, onion powder, and cayenne. Toss to coat the tofu. Allow to set for 5 minutes, turning once.

Step 3

Put panko on a plate. Coat both sides of the tofu with panko.

Step 4

Heat 3 tablespoons oil in a sizable nonstick skillet over medium-high heat. Add the tofu and cook until nicely browned on one side, 3 - 5 minutes. Drizzle the remaining 2 tablespoons oil over the tofu. Cook until the opposite end is browned, about 4 minutes more.

Step 5

Sprinkle the remaining ¼ teaspoon salt over the tofu and serve with the collards and hot honey, if desired.

Nutritional Info

Per Serving:

356 Calories; Protein 16.5g; Carbohydrates 20g; Dietary Fiber 7g; Sugars 2.4g; Fat 26.9g; Saturated

Fat 3g; Cholesterol 0.8mg; Vitamin A In 5858IU; Vitamin C 40.3mg; Folate 156.5mcg; Calcium 569mg; Iron 2mg;

Magnesium 68mg; Potassium 414mg; Sodium 510mg

Day 3

Chilean Lentil Stew with Salsa Verde

This nutritious vegetarian meal is delicious and filling. Don't skip the parsley relish (salsa verde)—it's simple to make and adds a tart touch to the lentil stew's tastes. For this stew, we like French green lentils because they don't fall apart when cooking; but, plain brown lentils (available in most supermarkets) will indeed work.

Recipe Summary

Active: 30 minutes | **Total: 40 minutes** | **Servings: 4**

Nutrition Profile:

Heart Healthy
Low-Calorie
High Fiber
Diabetes
Appropriate
Egg Free

Gluten-Free
Low Sodium
Nut-Free
High Blood
Pressure
Soy-Free

Healthy Aging
Healthy
Immunity
Healthy
Pregnancy

Ingredients

- 1 tablespoon olive oil
- 3 small carrots, peeled and finely chopped (½ cup)
- 1 ¼ cups finely chopped celery (4-6 stalks) or fennel (1 bulb)
- ½ cup finely chopped red bell pepper
- 1 ½ cups French green lentils, sorted and rinsed
- 5 tablespoons finely chopped shallot (1 large), divided
- 2 large cloves garlic, minced
- 2 tablespoons tomato paste
- ¾ teaspoon ground pepper, divided
- 4 cups low-sodium chicken broth or vegetable broth, or water
- ½ teaspoon salt, divided
- 1 small bunch Italian parsley, finely chopped (about 3/4 cup)
- 1 large lime, juiced (2 Tbsp.)
- 2 tablespoons white-wine vinegar

Instructions

Step 1

Heat oil in a 4- to 6-qt. Heat a saucepan over medium-high heat. Insert celery (or fennel), carrots, bell pepper, 3 Tbsp. shallot, and garlic. Cook, stirring constantly, for 3 minutes, or until softened. Cook, stirring constantly, for 30 seconds after adding tomato paste. Put lentils, broth (or water), ½ tsp. pepper, and ¼ teaspoon salt. Bring the mixture to a boil. Cover, lower heat to low, and simmer for 35 to 40 minutes, or until the lentils are cooked.

Step 2

Meanwhile, whisk together the parsley, lime juice, vinegar, and the remaining 2 tbsp. shallot and ¼ teaspoon in a small bowl, sprinkle the pepper and salt; whisk well.

Step 3

Distribute the stew among four bowls and top each with a dollop of the salsa verde. The remaining salsa verde should be served separately.

Tips
To prepare ahead of time: Prepare stew via Step 1. Store in the refrigerator for up to 3 days. Reheat on the oven or in the microwave, adding water if needed.

Nutritional Info
Per Serving:

321 Calories; Protein 18g; Carbohydrates 51g; Dietary Fiber 16g; Sugars 6g; Fat 5g; Saturated Fat 0.5g; Vitamin A In 8313IU; Vitamin C 46.3mg; Folate 43mcg; Calcium 83mg; Iron 5mg; Magnesium 20.2mg; Potassium 1011mg; Sodium 457mg

Day 4

Grilled Eggplant & Tomato Pasta

The flavor combination of slightly smoky grilled eggplant and sweet tomatoes is delectable. An easy, healthful midweek dinner is the eggplant-tomato mixture served over whole-wheat pasta with fresh basil and a sprinkle of salty cheese.

Recipe Summary

| Active: 30 minutes | Total: 30 minutes | Servings: 4 |

Nutrition Profile:

Heart Healthy	Low Sodium	Healthy Immunity
Low-Calorie	Nut-Free	Healthy Pregnancy
High Fiber	High Blood Pressure	Low Added Sugars
Diabetes Appropriate	Soy-Free	
Egg Free	Healthy Aging	
Vegetarian		

Ingredients

- 1 pound plum tomatoes, chopped
- 4 tablespoons extra-virgin olive oil, divided

- ½ teaspoon salt
- 2 teaspoons chopped fresh oregano
- ¼ teaspoon crushed red pepper
- 1 clove garlic, grated
- ½ teaspoon ground pepper
- 8 ounces whole-wheat penne
- 1 ½ pounds eggplant, cut into ½ -inch-thick slices
- ½ cup chopped fresh basil
- ¼ cup shaved ricotta salata or crumbled feta cheese

Instructions

Step 1

Bring a big pot of water to a boil. Preheat the grill to medium-high heat.

Step 2

Toss tomatoes with 3 tablespoons oil, oregano, garlic, pepper, crushed red pepper and salt in a huge bowl.

Step 3

Brush the remaining 1 tablespoon oil over the eggplant. Grill, rotating once, for 4 minutes per side, or until tender and charred in places. Allow for a 10-minute cooling period. Chop into bite-size pieces and combine with the tomatoes and basil.

Step 4

In the meantime, cook the pasta according to package guidelines. Drain.

Step 5

Serve the tomato sauce over the pasta. Garnish with cheese.

Nutritional Info

Per Serving:

450 Calories;
Protein 13g;
Carbohydrates
61g; Dietary Fiber
12g; Sugars 10g;
Fat 19.2g;
Saturated Fat 3g;

Cholesterol
8.3mg; Vitamin A
In 1374.2IU;
Vitamin C 21mg;
Folate 97mcg;
Calcium 107mg;
Iron 3mg;

Magnesium
125.9mg;
Potassium
840mg; Sodium
394mg

Day 5

Stuffed Potatoes with Salsa & Beans

With this easy dish of loaded baked potatoes with salsa, beans, and avocado, taco night meets baked potato night. This quick, healthy family dinner takes only 10 minutes to prepare, making it ideal for even the busiest weeknights. This recipe works just as well with sweet potatoes instead of russets.

Recipe Summary

Active: 10 minutes	Total: 25 minutes	Servings: 4

Nutrition Profile:

Heart Healthy	High Fiber	Egg Free
Low-Calorie	Dairy-Free	Gluten-Free
Low Carbohydrate	Diabetes Appropriate	Vegetarian Vegan

• • •

Low Sodium
Nut-Free

High Blood
Pressure
Soy-Free

Low Added
Sugars

Ingredients

- 4 medium russet potatoes
- ½ cup fresh salsa
- A ripe avocado, sliced
- 1 (15 ounce) can pinto beans, rinsed, warmed and lightly mashed
- 4 teaspoons chopped pickled jalapeños

Instructions

Step 1

Pierce sweet potatoes all over with a fork. Microwave on Medium for about 20 minutes, rotating one or twice. (Alternatively, bake potatoes at 425°F for 45 minutes to 1 hour, or until soft.) Allow to cool gently on a clean cutting board.

Step 2

To open the potato, make a lengthwise cut with a kitchen towel to protect your hands, but don't cut all the way through. Pinch the ends together to expose the flesh.

Step 3

Garnish each potato with salsa, avocado, beans, and jalapeos. Serve hot.

Nutritional Info

Per Serving:

324 Calories;
Protein 9.2g;
Carbohydrates
56.7g; Dietary
Fiber 11g; Sugars
5g; Fat 8g;
Saturated Fat

1.2g; Vitamin A
In 190.8IU;
Vitamin C
21.2mg; Folate
104.8mcg;
Calcium 74mg;
Iron 3mg;

Magnesium
92.8mg;
Potassium
1455mg; Sodium
421mg

Day 6

Mediterranean Broccoli Pasta Salad

This healthful pasta salad is rich with vegetables and Mediterranean flavors. The dressing is flavored with sun-dried tomatoes and lemon zest, and tender-crisp broccoli florets simmer alongside the pasta, making assembling (and cleanup!) a snap.

Recipe Summary

| Active: 25 minutes | Total: 25 minutes | Servings: 10 |

Nutrition Profile:

Heart Healthy	Vegetarian	Soy-Free
Diabetes	Low Sodium	Healthy
Appropriate	Nut-Free	Immunity

Ingredients

- 8 ounces whole-wheat farfalle pasta
- 6 cups broccoli florets
- ½ cup chopped red bell pepper
- 2 tablespoons chopped fresh basil
- ½ teaspoon salt
- ¼ cup chopped red onion

- 2 tablespoons chopped fresh flat-leaf parsley
- ¾ cup mayonnaise
- 1 teaspoon lemon zest
- ½ cup finely chopped sun-dried tomatoes in oil, drained
- 1 teaspoon dried oregano
- ¼ teaspoon crushed red pepper

Instructions

Step 1

Keep a large dish of ice water close to the stove. Bring a big pot of water to a boil. Cook the pasta according to the package recommendations, adding the broccoli to the water in the last 2 minutes of cooking time. Drain the pasta and broccoli and place them in a bowl of ice water. Drain thoroughly. Transfer to a large mixing bowl; stir in the bell pepper, onion, parsley, and basil.

Step 2

In a small mixing bowl, combine mayonnaise, sun-dried tomatoes, lemon zest, oregano, salt, and crushed red pepper. Toss into the pasta mixture to coat.

To prepare ahead of time: Refrigerate for up to 1 day in an airtight container.

Nutritional Info

Per Serving:

212 Calories;	Dietary Fiber 3g;	Cholesterol 7mg;
Protein 5g;	Sugars 1g; Fat 13g;	Vitamin A In
Carbohydrates 21g;	Saturated Fat 2.1g;	1704.6IU; Vitamin C

56mg; Folate
52mcg; Calcium

38mg; Iron 1.5mg;
Magnesium 55mg;

Potassium 312mg;
Sodium 255mg

Day 7

Vegetarian Lo Mein with Shiitakes, Carrots & Bean Sprouts

This nutritious vegetarian meal gets a sweet and spicy kick from Sriracha. Fresh lo mein noodles, which may be obtained in Asian markets, are used in traditional lo mein. You can alternatively use fresh or dried linguine noodles (fresh linguine can be found in the refrigerated department of some supermarkets). This quick dinner takes only 30 minutes to prepare and is ideal for weeknights.

Recipe Summary

Active: 30 minutes | **Total: 30 minutes** | **Servings: 4**

Nutrition Profile:

Heart Healthy	**Diabetes**	**Vegan**
Low-Calorie	**Appropriate**	**Low Sodium**
Dairy-Free	**Egg Free**	**Nut-Free**
	Vegetarian	**Healthy Aging**

Ingredients

- 8 ounces fresh lo mein noodles or fresh or dried linguine pasta
- 2 teaspoons Sriracha
- 2 teaspoons toasted sesame oil
- 3 tablespoons reduced-sodium soy sauce
- 2 tablespoons minced garlic

• • •

- 2 cups bean sprouts
- 2 tablespoons vegetable oil, divided
- 1 large carrot, halved lengthwise and cut into ¼ -inch-thick half-moon slices (about 1 cup)
- 4 ounces fresh shiitake mushrooms, stems removed, caps sliced ¼ -inch thick
- 1 cup thinly sliced celery
- 3 tablespoons finely chopped fresh cilantro

Instructions

Step 1

Bring a big pot of water to a boil. Cook the noodles according to the package instructions. Drain the noodles, rinse with cold water, and shake off excess water until totally dry (pat noodles dry if needed). Toss with sesame oil in a large mixing basin and set aside. In a small bowl, combine the soy sauce and Sriracha; set aside.

Step 2

Heat a 14-inch flat-bottomed carbon-steel wok (or 12-inch stainless-steel skillet) over high heat until a drop of water vaporizes in 1–2 seconds. Sprinkle in 1 Tbsp. vegetable oil. Add the garlic; stir-fry until just aromatic, just around 10 seconds. Stir in the carrot, mushrooms, and celery for approximately 1 minute, or until the celery is brilliant green and the veggies have absorbed all of the oil.

Step 3

Swirl in the remaining 1 tablespoon of vegetable oil. Stir in the bean sprouts, noodles, and soy sauce mixture for 1 to 2 minutes, or until the noodles are heated through and the vegetables are tender-crisp. Toss in the cilantro to mix.

Tips

Devices: 14-inch flat-bottomed carbon-steel wok or 12-inch stainless-steel skillet

Nutritional Info

Per Serving:
309 Calories; Protein 12g; Carbohydrates 41.1g; Dietary Fiber 4g; Sugars 5g; Fat 11g; Saturated Fat **1.4g; Cholesterol 26.7mg; Vitamin A In 3265.6IU; Vitamin C 9.8mg; Folate 49.5mcg; Calcium** **39mg; Iron 1.5mg; Magnesium 21mg; Potassium 648mg; Sodium 552mg**

Day 8

Curried Sweet Potato & Peanut Soup

Sweet potatoes simmer in a fast coconut curry in this delectable soup recipe, producing in a creamy, rich broth flecked with garlic and ginger flavors. We enjoy peanuts because of their low cost and diverse flavor. They're also high in protein, with 7 grams per ounce.

Recipe Summary

Active: 35 minutes   **Total: 40 minutes**   **Servings: 6**

Nutrition Profile:

Heart Healthy   **Dairy-Free**   **Vegetarian**
Low-Calorie   **Diabetes**   **Vegan**
High Fiber   **Appropriate**   **Low Sodium**

● ● ●

Soy-Free
Healthy Aging

Low Added
Sugars

Ingredients

- 2 tablespoons canola oil
- 3 cups water
- 1 ½ cups diced yellow onion
- 1 tablespoon minced garlic
- 1 tablespoon minced fresh ginger
- 4 teaspoons red curry paste (see Tip)
- 1 serrano chile, ribs and seeds removed, minced
- 1 pound sweet potatoes, peeled and cubed (½ -inch pieces)
- 1 cup "lite" coconut milk
- ¾ teaspoon salt
- ¾ cup unsalted dry-roasted peanuts
- 1 (15 ounce) can white beans, rinsed
- ¼ teaspoon ground pepper
- ¼ cup chopped fresh cilantro
- Lime wedges
- 2 tablespoons lime juice
- ¼ cup unsalted roasted pumpkin seeds

Instructions

Step 1

In a big pot, heat the oil over medium-high heat. Insert onion, and sauté stirring often, until softened and translucent, about 4 minutes.

Step 2

Stir in minced garlic, ginger, curry paste, and serrano; cook, stirring, for 1 minute. Stir in potatoes and water; bring to a boil. Lower the heat to medium-low and simmer, slightly covered, for 8 - 10 minutes, or until the sweet potatoes are tender.

Step 3

Puree half of the soup, along with the coconut milk and peanuts, in a blender. (Be careful when pureeing hot liquids.) Bring it back to the pot with the remaining soup. Stir in beans, salt, and pepper; heat through. Take the pan off the heat. Stirring in cilantro and lime juice. Garnish with pumpkin seeds and lime wedges.

Tips

Red curry paste can be found in the Asian aisle of most supermarkets, packaged in a small glass container.

To prepare ahead of time: Soup can be stored in the refrigerator for up to 3 days. Heat it up before serving.

Nutritional Info

Per Serving:

342 Calories;	14g; Saturated Fat	87.9mg; Iron 2mg;
Protein 12g;	4.3g; Vitamin A In	Magnesium 90mg;
Carbohydrates	10785IU; Vitamin C	Potassium 692mg;
37.4g; Dietary Fiber	7.5mg; Folate	Sodium 597mg
8g; Sugars 8g; Fat	95mcg; Calcium	

Day 9

Zucchini-Chickpea Veggie Burgers with Tahini-Ranch Sauce

You'll want to prepare this vegan burger recipe repeatedly. For a filling and healthful homemade vegetarian burger, savory chickpea and zucchini patties are topped with a creamy, herb-flecked tahini ranch sauce, juicy tomato slices, and peppery arugula. Serve them on buns or in pita wraps. We recommend making extra sauce since it makes an excellent dip for veggie sticks and a superb salad dressing when thinned with a little water.

Recipe Summary

Active: 25 minutes	**Total: 25 minutes**	**Servings: 4**

Nutrition Profile:

Heart Healthy	Diabetes	Low Sodium
Low-Calorie	Appropriate	Nut-Free
High Fiber	Egg Free	Healthy Aging
Dairy-Free	Vegetarian	Healthy
	Vegan	Immunity

Ingredients

- 4 tablespoons tahini, divided
- 1 tablespoon lemon juice
- 3 teaspoons white miso, divided
- 2 tablespoons water
- 1 ¼ teaspoons onion powder, divided
- 1 ¼ teaspoons garlic powder, divided
- 1 ¼ teaspoons ground pepper, divided
- ¼ teaspoon salt

- 1 teaspoon chopped fresh chives plus 2 tablespoons, divided
- 1 (15 ounce) can no-salt-added chickpeas, rinsed
- 1 teaspoon ground cumin
- ¼ cup fresh parsley leaves
- ½ cup shredded zucchini
- ⅓ cup old-fashioned rolled oats
- 4 slices tomato
- 1 tablespoon extra-virgin olive oil
- 4 whole-grain hamburger buns, toasted
- 1 cup packed fresh arugula

Instructions

Step 1

In a small mixing bowl, combine 2 tablespoons tahini, lemon juice, 1 teaspoon miso, ½ teaspoon onion powder, ¼ teaspoon garlic powder, and ¼ teaspoon pepper. Whisk in the water gradually until the mixture is smooth. Sprinkle in 1 tsp chives. Place aside.

Step 2

In a food processor, combine chickpeas, cumin, salt, and the remaining 2 tablespoons tahini, 2 teaspoons miso, 1 teaspoon garlic powder, 1 teaspoon pepper, and 3/4 teaspoon onion powder. Pulse until a gritty mixture develops that holds together when squeezed, stopping once or twice to wipe down the edges. Pulse in the parsley and remaining 2 tablespoons chives until the herbs are finely chopped and mixed into the mixture. Transfer to a bowl.

Step 3

Squeeze zucchini in a hygienic kitchen towel to remove extra moisture. Add the zucchini and oats to the chickpea mixture and mash together with your fingertips. Form the mixture into 4 patties.

Step 4

Heat the oil nonstick skillet over medium-high heat. Simply add the patties and fry until golden and starts to crisp, 4 to 5 minutes. Cook until golden brown, 2–4 minutes more.

Step 5

Serve the burgers with the tahini-ranch sauce, arugula, and tomato slices on buns.

Tips

To prepare ahead of time: The burger patties and tahini ranch sauce can be made ahead of time. Prepare through Step 3; refrigerate for up to 24 hours, covered individually.

Nutritional Info

Per Serving:

303 Calories;
Protein 12.9g;
Carbohydrates
47g; Dietary Fiber
9.g; Sugars 5g;
Fat 14g;
Saturated Fat

2.1g; Vitamin A
In 724.3IU;
Vitamin C
14.6mg; Folate
51.8mcg; Calcium
139.9mg; Iron
3mg; Magnesium

91mg; Potassium
527mg; Sodium
537mg; Thiamin
0.4mg

Day 10

Fattoush Salad

Red cabbage gives this fattoush salad extra crunch.

Recipe Summary

Active: 25 minutes	**Total: 25 minutes**	**Servings: 8**

Nutrition Profile:

Heart Healthy	**Diabetes**	**Nut-Free**
Low-Calorie	**Appropriate**	**Soy-Free**
Low	**Egg Free**	**Healthy**
Carbohydrate	**Vegetarian**	**Immunity**
High Fiber	**Vegan**	**Low Added**
Dairy-Free	**Low Sodium**	**Sugars**

Ingredients

- 2 whole-wheat pita breads, split and torn into 1-inch pieces
- ¼ cup lemon juice
- ½ teaspoon ground pepper
- 3 tablespoons extra-virgin olive oil
- ½ teaspoon kosher salt
- 1 cup grape or cherry tomatoes, halved
- 3 cups thinly sliced red cabbage
- 3 cups chopped romaine lettuce
- 2 Persian cucumbers, sliced
- 2 scallions, thinly sliced
- 1 cup chopped fresh parsley

Instructions

● ● ●

Step 1

Preheat oven to 375 degrees F.

Step 2

Arrange pita pieces on a large rimmed baking sheet in a single layer. Bake, tossing once, for (10 - 15 minutes or until crisp. Let chill to room temperature, about 5 minutes.

Step 3

Meanwhile, in a large mixing bowl, combine the lemon juice, oil, salt, and pepper. Put cabbage, lettuce, tomatoes, cucumbers, scallions and parsley and toss. Insert the pita chips and toss until mixed.

Nutritional Info

Per Serving:

119 Calories;	Saturated Fat 0.8g;	26mg; Iron 0.8mg;
Protein 2g;	Vitamin A In	Magnesium 26mg;
Carbohydrates 14g;	2364.8IU; Vitamin C	Potassium 186mg;
Dietary Fiber 2g;	23.5mg; Folate	Sodium 166mg
Sugars 2g; Fat 5g;	48mcg; Calcium	

Day 11

Chinese Sweet & Sour Tofu Stir-Fry with Snow Peas

This nutritious sweet and sour tofu stir-fry comes together quickly on weeknights. Just make sure to plan ahead of time so that you can freeze the tofu. This gives the tofu a meatier mouthfeel and helps it soak up the sauce.

Recipe Summary

Active: 30 minutes   **Total: 2 days**   **Servings: 4**

Nutrition Profile:

Heart Healthy	**Egg Free**	**High Calcium**
Low-Calorie	**Vegetarian**	**Bone Health**
Dairy-Free	**Vegan**	**Healthy Aging**
Diabetes	**Low Sodium**	
Appropriate	**Nut-Free**	

Ingredients

- 1 (14 ounce) package water-packed firm tofu
- ⅔ cup pineapple juice
- ½ cup ketchup
- 2 tablespoons vegetable oil
- 1 tablespoon reduced-sodium soy sauce
- 8 ounces snow peas (4 ¼ cups), trimmed
- 1 tablespoon cornstarch
- 1 tablespoon minced fresh ginger
- 2 tablespoons thinly sliced scallions

Instructions

Step 1

Drain and rinse the tofu one to three days before cooking. Wrap in foil and place in the freezer for at least 3 - 4 hours, or until solid. Set the tofu in a bowl and place it in the refrigerator to defrost overnight the day before cooking.

Step 2

Put the thawed tofu on a plate propped with a double layer of paper towels. Cover with 2 more paper towels, add a plate on top, and place a weight on the plate, such as 2 cans of beans. Allow for a 20-minute resting period.

Step 3

Mix pineapple juice, ketchup, and soy sauce in a small bowl; cast aside.

Step 4

Slice the pressed tofu into 12 slices, a scant ½ inch thick. Gently dust both sides with cornstarch.

Step 5

Heat a 12-inch stainless steel griddle (or 14-inch flat-bottomed carbon-steel wok; over high heat until a drop of water vaporizes within 1–2 seconds of contact. Swirl in the oil, then reduce to medium heat and add the tofu in an even layer. Cook for 1 minute, or until the bottom is light golden. Flip sides, sprinkle with ginger, and cook for 1 minute more, or until the second side is light golden.

Step 6

Take the pan off the heat. Stir in the snow peas and the reserved sauce. Cover and set aside for 30 seconds, or until the sauce stops sizzling. Return the pan to medium heat and stir-fry for 1 to 2 minutes, or until the sauce is thoroughly spread and the peas are tender-crisp. Serve with scallions.

Tip

If you don't have a well-seasoned carbon-steel wok, use a stainless-steel skillet. The acidity of the pineapple juice and ketchup will erase the patina from a new wok; the patina of a well-seasoned wok will return with continued cooking.

Cooking tools: 12" stainless-steel skillet or well-seasoned 14" flat-bottomed carbon-steel wok

Nutritional Info

Per Serving:

215 Calories;
Protein 11g;
Carbohydrates 21g;
Dietary Fiber 2g;
Sugars 12g; Fat

13g; Saturated Fat
1.8g; Vitamin A In
308.3IU; Vitamin C
32.8mg; Folate
47mcg; Calcium

231mg; Iron 2mg;
Magnesium 53mg;
Potassium 444mg;
Sodium 502mg

Day 12

Kale & Roasted Sweet Potato Hash

This one-pan hash is perfect for a quick fall meal or a simple dish for a nutritious brunch. You may also poach the eggs ahead of time and then rewarm them in hot water right before serving.

Recipe Summary

Active: 20 minutes   **Total: 35 minutes**   **Servings: 4**

• • •

Nutrition Profile:

Heart Healthy	Gluten-Free	Soy-Free
Low-Calorie	Vegetarian	Healthy
Diabetes	Low Sodium	Immunity
Appropriate	Nut-Free	

Ingredients

- 1 medium red onion, halved and sliced
- 1 pound sweet potatoes (about 2 small or 1 large), peeled and cut into ½ -inch pieces (3 ½ cups)
- 4 large eggs
- Pinch salt, divided
- 2 tablespoons canola oil, divided
- 1 teaspoon garlic powder
- 4 cups chopped kale
- Freshly ground pepper to taste

Instructions

Step 1

Arrange a large rimmed baking sheet in the oven; preheat oven to 415 degrees F.

Step 2

In a medium mixing dish, combine sweet potatoes and onion with 1 tablespoon oil, ½ teaspoon garlic powder, and ¼ teaspoon salt. Spread in a uniform layer on the heated baking tray. Roast for 20 minutes.

Step 3

Toss the kale with the remaining 1 tablespoon of oil, ½ teaspoon garlic powder, and ¼ teaspoon salt. Remove the pan from the oven, toss in the vegetables, and top with the kale. Continue roasting for another 10 minutes, or until the sweet potatoes have softened and started to brown and the kale is wilted and somewhat crunchy. Stir to combine.

Step 4

Meanwhile, bring 2 inches of water to a boil in a large pot. Lower heat to medium-low to sustain a gentle simmer. Break each egg into a small bowl and carefully place it in the simmering water, being careful not to break the yolks. Poach for 4 minutes if you want soft-set, 5 minutes if you want medium-set, and 8 minutes if you want hard-set. Using a slotted spoon, remove the eggs to a clean kitchen towel to drain.

Step 5

Divide the vegetable hash among four plates, topping each with an egg. Season with pepper, if needed.

Nutritional Info

Per Serving:

207 calories; protein 8g; carbohydrates 12g; dietary fiber 3g; sugars 6.2g; fat 12g; saturated fat 2.1g; cholesterol 186mg; vitamin a in 15127.7IU; vitamin c 34.8mg; folate 58mcg; calcium 85.3mg; iron 1.7mg; magnesium 35.5mg; potassium 527mg; sodium 392mg

Day 13

Mushroom & Tofu Stir-Fry

This tofu veggie stir-fry is quick and easy to make, making it an excellent weeknight meal. Baked tofu does have a firm, toothsome crunchiness that crisps well in a hot pan. It comes in teriyaki and sesame tastes, both of which are wonderful. Alternatively, go for a smoked version, which has the same texture but a stronger flavor. Serve over brown rice.

Recipe Summary

Active: 20 minutes   Total: 20 minutes   Servings: 5

Nutrition Profile:

Heart Healthy	Diabetes	Low Sodium
Low-Calorie	Appropriate	Soy-Free
Low	Egg Free	Low Added
Carbohydrate	Gluten-Free	Sugars
Dairy-Free	Vegetarian	

Ingredients

- 4 tablespoons peanut oil or canola oil, divided
- 1 pound mixed mushrooms, sliced
- 1 medium red bell pepper, diced
- 1 bunch scallions, trimmed and cut into 2-inch pieces
- 1 tablespoon grated fresh ginger
- 1 large clove garlic, grated
- 1 (8 ounce) container baked tofu or smoked tofu, diced
- 3 tablespoons oyster sauce or vegetarian oyster sauce

Instructions

Step 1

In a big flat-bottom wok or cast-iron skillet, heat 2 tablespoons oil over high heat. Add mushrooms and bell pepper; fry, stirring every once in a while until tender, about 4 minutes. Cook for another 30 seconds after adding the scallions, ginger, and garlic. Place the vegetables in a bowl.

Step 2

Add remaining 2 tablespoons oil and tofu to the pan. Cook, rotating once, for 3 to 4 minutes, or until browned. Gently stir in the vegetables and oyster sauce. Cook, stirring constantly, until heated, about 1 minute.

Tip

Swap vegetarian oyster or stir-fry sauce, if required, which uses mushrooms instead of oysters.

Nutritional Info

Per Serving:
170 Calories; Protein 7g; Carbohydrates 6g; Dietary Fiber 3g; Sugars 3g; Fat 13g; Saturated Fat 3g; Vitamin A In 924.7IU; Vitamin C 36mg; Folate 43mcg; Calcium 113mg; Iron 1.6mg; Magnesium 35mg; Potassium 467mg; Sodium 302mg

Spinach Salad with Roasted Sweet Potatoes, White Beans & Basil

In this healthful main dish salad, roasted sweet potatoes are combined with spinach, cabbage, and white beans and mixed with a bright basil dressing.

Recipe Summary

Active: 40 minutes   **Total: 40 minutes**   **Servings: 4**

Nutrition Profile:

Heart Healthy	Egg Free	Healthy Aging
Low-Calorie	Gluten-Free	Healthy
High Fiber	Vegetarian	Immunity
Dairy-Free	Vegan	
Diabetes	Low Sodium	
Appropriate	Soy-Free	

Ingredients

- 1 sweet potato (12 ounces), peeled and diced (½ -inch)
- ¼ teaspoon salt, divided
- 5 tablespoons extra-virgin olive oil, divided
- ½ teaspoon ground pepper, divided
- ½ cup packed fresh basil leaves
- 3 tablespoons cider vinegar
- 10 cups baby spinach
- 1 tablespoon finely chopped shallot
- 2 teaspoons whole-grain mustard
- 1 (15 ounce) can low-sodium cannellini beans, rinsed
- 2 cups shredded cabbage
- 1 cup chopped red bell pepper
- ⅓ cup chopped pecans, toasted

Instructions

Step 1

Preheat oven to 425 degrees F.

Step 2

Toss sweet potatoes, 1 tablespoon oil, ¼ teaspoon pepper and 1/8 teaspoon salt together in a large mixing bowl. Transfer to a large rimmed baking sheet and roast, stirring once, for 16 - 20 minutes, or until soft. Allow to cool for at least 10 minutes.

Step 3

Meanwhile, in a little food processor, combine basil, the remaining ¼ cup oil, vinegar, shallot, mustard, and the remaining ¼ teaspoon pepper and 1/8 teaspoon salt. Blend until nearly smooth. Transfer to a large mixing bowl. Mix in the spinach, beans, cabbage, bell pepper, pecans, and cooled sweet potatoes. Toss to coat.

Nutritional Info

Per Serving:
405 Calories; Protein 11g; Carbohydrates 44.3g; Dietary Fiber 14.7g; Sugars 7g; Fat 23.6g; Saturated Fat 2g; Vitamin A In 22749.1IU; Vitamin C 103.7mg; Folate 48mcg; Calcium 191mg; Iron 5mg; Magnesium 149mg; Potassium 491mg; Sodium 545mg

Day 15

Summer Skillet Vegetable & Egg Scramble

Don't discard out those almost-worn-out vegetables and fresh herbs. Toss them into this skillet egg scramble for a quick vegetarian dinner. Almost any vegetable will work in this simple skillet dish, so use your favorites or whatever vegetables you have on hand.

Recipe Summary

Active: 30 minutes	Total: 30 minutes	Servings: 4

Nutrition Profile:

Heart Healthy	Vegetarian	Healthy
Low-Calorie	Low Sodium	Immunity
Dairy-Free	Nut-Free	Low Added
Diabetes	High Blood	Sugars
Appropriate	Pressure	
Gluten-Free	Soy-Free	

Ingredients

- 2 tablespoons olive oil
- 3 scallions, thinly sliced, green and white parts separated
- 12 ounces baby potatoes, thinly sliced
- 4 cups thinly sliced vegetables, such as mushrooms, bell peppers, and/or zucchini (14 oz.)
- 1 teaspoon minced fresh herbs, such as rosemary or thyme
- 2 cups packed leafy greens, such as baby spinach or baby kale (2 oz.)

- 6 large eggs (or 4 large eggs plus 4 egg whites), lightly beaten
- ½ teaspoon salt

Instructions

Step 1

In a large cast-iron or nonstick skillet, heat the oil over medium heat. Cover and cook, stirring occasionally, until the potatoes begin to soften, about 8-10 minutes

Step 2

Add the sliced veggies and scallion whites and simmer, uncovered, for 8 - 10 minutes or until the vegetables are soft and lightly browned. Add the herbs and mix well. Place the veggie mixture around the pan's edge.

Step 3

Reduce heat to medium-low. In the center of the pan, place the eggs and scallion greens. Cook, stirring constantly, for about 2 minutes, or until the eggs are lightly scrambled.

Step 4

Toss the eggs with the leafy greens. Remove from the heat and mix thoroughly to blend. Add the salt and mix well.

Nutritional Info

Per Serving:

254 Calories;
Protein 12.4g;
Carbohydrates
19.7g; Dietary
Fiber 4.3g; Sugars
4.5g; Fat 14.2g;

Saturated Fat
3.3g; Cholesterol
279mg; Vitamin
A In 2932IU;
Vitamin C 87mg;
Folate 73mcg;

Calcium 72mg;
Iron 2mg;
Magnesium
36mg; Potassium
718mg; Sodium
415mg

Day 16

Banh Mi Black Rice Bowls

We got inspired by the popular Vietnamese banh mi sandwich for this fast dinner meal, but we left off the bun to make way for one of our favorite whole grains: black (aka forbidden) rice. Simply replace the fish sauce with more tamari to make these wholesome grain bowls vegetarian.

Recipe Summary

Active: 30 minutes   **Total: 45 minutes**   **Servings: 4**

Nutrition Profile:

Heart Healthy	Egg Free	High Calcium
Low-Calorie	Gluten-Free	Bone Health
Dairy-Free	Vegetarian	Healthy Aging
Diabetes	Low Sodium	Low Added
Appropriate	Nut-Free	Sugars

Ingredients

- 1 cup black rice, rinsed
- ½ cup rice vinegar
- 2 cups water
- 1 teaspoon honey
- 1 teaspoon salt, divided

- 2 teaspoons fish sauce or tamari
- 1 tablespoon toasted sesame oil
- 1 tablespoon reduced-sodium tamari
- 1 (14 ounce) package firm water-packed tofu, cubed
- 1 tablespoon sugar
- ½ cup shredded red cabbage
- 1 cup julienned carrot
- 1 cup julienned daikon radish
- ¼ cup fresh mint and/or cilantro
- Sriracha mayo & sliced jalapeño for garnish

Instructions

Step 1

Combine rice, water and ¼ teaspoon salt in a medium saucepan. Bring the mixture to a boil over high heat. Reduce the heat to maintain a slow simmer, cover, and cook for 30 minutes, or until the rice is tender. Remove from the heat and let aside for 5 minutes, covered.

Step 2

Meanwhile, combine oil, tamari, fish sauce (or more tamari) and honey in a medium bowl. Toss in the tofu to coat. Allow to cool to room temperature, stirring occasionally.

Step 3

In a medium mixing bowl, combine the vinegar, sugar, and the remaining 3/4 teaspoon salt. Allow carrot and daikon to stand for 10 minutes. Remove and discard the liquid.
Step 4

Distribute the rice, tofu, marinated vegetables and cabbage among 4 serving bowls, topped with herbs, Sriracha mayo and jalapeño, as desired.

Nutritional Info

Per Serving:

323 Calories; Protein 12g; Carbohydrates 43g; Dietary Fiber 6g; Sugars 4g; Fat 11g; Saturated

Fat 1g; Vitamin A In 3785IU; Vitamin C 7.5mg; Folate 18.5mcg; Calcium 216.7mg; Iron 3.8mg;

Magnesium 16.6mg; Potassium 161.2mg; Sodium 489mg

Day 17

Quinoa, Avocado & Chickpea Salad over Mixed Greens

Quinoa and chickpeas supply protein to this spicy and nutritious salad recipe.

Recipe Summary

Active: 30 minutes   Total: 35 minutes   Servings: 2

Nutrition Profile:

Heart Healthy   Dairy-Free   Low Sodium
High Fiber   Gluten-Free   Nutrition Info

Ingredients

- ⅓ cup quinoa
- ⅔ cup water
- ¼ teaspoon kosher salt or other coarse salt
- 3 tablespoons olive oil

• • •

- 1 clove garlic, crushed and peeled
- 2 teaspoons grated lemon zest
- 3 tablespoons lemon juice
- ¼ teaspoon ground pepper
- ½ avocado, diced
- 1 cup rinsed no-salt-added canned chickpeas
- 1 medium carrot, shredded (½ cup)
- 1 (5 ounce) package prewashed mixed greens, such as spring mix or baby kale-spinach blend (8 cups packed)

Instructions

Step 1

Bring water to a boil in a small saucepan. Mix in the quinoa. Reduce the heat to low, cover, and simmer for 15 minutes, or until all of the liquid has been absorbed. Allow to cool for 5 minutes after fluffing and separating the grains with a fork.

Step 2

Meanwhile, season the garlic on a cutting board with salt. Mash the garlic with the back of a spoon until it forms a paste. Scrape into a medium mixing bowl. Stir in lemon zest, lemon juice, oil, and pepper. Set aside 3 tablespoons of the dressing in a small bowl.

Step 3

Toss the chickpeas, carrot, and avocado with the remaining dressing in the bowl. Allow flavors to combine for 5 minutes before serving. Gently mix in the quinoa to coat.

Step 4

Toss the greens in a large mixing bowl with the reserved 3 Tbsp. dressing. Top the greens with the quinoa mixture and divide between two plates.

Tips

To make ahead, prepare the quinoa (Step 1) and store in the refrigerator for up to 2 days.

Nutritional Info

Per Serving:

500 Calories;	Saturated Fat	Iron 3.5mg;
Protein 12g;	4.3g; Vitamin A	Magnesium
Carbohydrates	In 7120.5IU;	111mg;
43g; Dietary Fiber	Vitamin C 32mg;	Potassium
12g; Sugars 6g;	Folate 216.1mcg;	844.2mg; Sodium
Fat 31g;	Calcium 111.4mg;	345mg

Day 18

Eggplant Tortilla Casserole

This layered casserole is inspired by famous cheese enchiladas, but without the hassle of rolling and stuffing individual tortillas. You'd never realize that this hearty Tex-Mex casserole contains a layer of thinly sliced eggplant. When roasted, the thin slices become soft and offer a mild savory aroma.

Recipe Summary

Active: 30 minutes   Total: 1 hr. 10 minutes Servings: 8

Heart Healthy	Gluten-Free	Bone Health
Low-Calorie	Vegetarian	Healthy Aging
High Fiber	Low Sodium	Low Added
Diabetes	Nut-Free	Sugars
Appropriate	High Calcium	
Egg Free	Soy-Free	

Ingredients

- 1 medium eggplant (about 1 lb.)
- 2 tablespoons canola oil, divided
- 1 tablespoon chili powder
- 2 medium onions, thinly sliced
- 3 cloves garlic, minced
- 1 teaspoon ground cumin
- 2 teaspoons dried oregano
- 1 teaspoon onion powder
- 1 (28 ounce) can no-salt-added diced tomatoes
- 10 corn tortillas, quartered
- 2 (15 ounce) cans no-salt-added black beans, rinsed
- 2 (4.5 ounce) cans mild green chiles
- ¼ cup chopped fresh cilantro
- 1 cup shredded extra-sharp Cheddar cheese

Instructions

Step 1

Preheat oven to 375 degrees F. Grease a large rimmed baking sheet and two 8-inch-square baking dishes with cooking spray.

Step 2

Peel the eggplant and cut into ¼ -inch-thick rounds. Cut the rounds in half (or quarter, if large). Arrange in a single layer on a baking sheet lined with parchment paper; brush with 1 tbsp. Pour the oil over the eggplant. Bake, rotating once, for 10 to 15 minutes, or until the eggplant is just starts to brown on the edges. Allow to cool.

Step 3

Heat the remaining 1 Tbsp. oil in a sizeable non - stick saucepan over medium heat. Cook, stirring occasionally, until the onions are soft, about 10 minutes. Insert garlic, chili powder, oregano, onion powder, and cumin; continue cooking just until aromatic, about 30 seconds. Pour in tomatoes, beans, chiles, and cilantro. Place aside.

Step 4

To make the casseroles, cover the bottom of each baking dish with ¼ of the tortilla pieces. Spread 1 cup of the tomato-bean mixture onto each tortilla, then top with ¼ cup Cheddar. Top each with ½ of the eggplant pieces, followed by 1 cup of the tomato-bean mixture.

Step 5

Distribute the remaining tortilla pieces and tomato-bean mixture among the casseroles, then top with ¼ cup Cheddar. Wrap foil around both dishes. One casserole can be labeled and frozen for up to a month.

Step 6

Bake the remaining casserole for 30 minutes, or until it is bubbling.

Step 7

Uncover and bake for another 10 minutes, or until the cheese is lightly browned. Allow for a 5-minute rest before slicing.

Tips

To prepare ahead of time: This double-batch recipe yields one dish for tonight and one that may be frozen for up to one month (Step 4). Cooking from frozen: Thaw in the refrigerator overnight before baking as suggested in Steps 5-6.

Cook equipment: Two 8-inch square baking dishes or foil pans are required.

Nutritional Info

Per Serving:
314 Calories; Protein 12g; Carbohydrates 41.3g; Dietary Fiber 10g; Sugars 7g; Fat 10g; Saturated Fat 3g; Cholesterol 12.7mg; Vitamin A In 925.8iu; Vitamin C 35.2mg; Folate 20mcg; Calcium 213mg; Iron 3mg; Magnesium 84.3mg; Potassium 487mg; Sodium 251mg

Day 19

Tex-Mex Pasta Salad

This simple pasta salad with Southwestern tastes is enhanced with a light and creamy green-salsa dressing.

Recipe Summary

Active: 10 minutes   Total: 15 minutes   Servings: 1

Nutrition Profile:

Heart Healthy	Low Sodium	Healthy
Low-Calorie	Nut-Free	Immunity
High Fiber	High Blood	Healthy
Diabetes	Pressure	Pregnancy
Appropriate	High Calcium	Low Added
Egg Free	Bone Health	Sugars
Vegetarian	Healthy Aging	

Ingredients

- 1 tablespoon tomatillo salsa
- ¾ cup chopped red bell pepper
- 1 tablespoon low-fat plain Greek yogurt
- 1 cup cherry tomatoes, halved
- ⅛ teaspoon salt
- ¾ cup frozen shelled edamame (4 oz.), cooked according to package directions, drained and cooled
- ½ cup cooked orzo, preferably whole-wheat, cooled
- ¼ cup chopped red onion
- 2 tablespoons shredded pepper Jack cheese
- ⅛ teaspoon ground pepper
- 1 tablespoon toasted pepitas
- Hot sauce, to taste
- Lime wedge, for serving

• • •

Instructions

Step 1

Whisk salsa and yogurt in a small bowl. Place aside.

Step 2

Combine tomatoes, bell pepper, edamame, orzo, onion, and cheese in a mixing bowl. Toss in the salt, pepper, and salsa dressing to blend. Season with hot sauce to taste, top with pepitas, and serve with a wedge of lime, if preferred.

Tips

Pepitas are pumpkin seeds, but they are not the same as the seeds you scrape out of your Halloween pumpkin: they are from pumpkin varietals that produce seeds without a strong outer hull. Pepitas can be found in bulk bins at natural food stores and large supermarkets, as well as online at nuts.com and elsewhere. To toast the pepitas, heat a small pan over medium heat and add the pepitas. Cook, stirring regularly, for 1 - 2 minutes, or until lightly browned.

To prepare ahead of time: Cook pasta up to 1 day ahead and refrigerate.

Nutritional Info

Per Serving:

404 Calories; Protein 24g; Carbohydrates 50.6g; Dietary Fiber 15.4g; Sugars 13g; Fat 12g; Saturated Fat 4g; Cholesterol 13mg; Vitamin A In 5078.8IU; Vitamin C 177.1mg; Folate 358.2mcg; Calcium 217mg; Iron 3mg; Magnesium 139mg; Potassium 1223mg; Sodium 502mg

Day 20

Vegan Roasted Vegetable Quinoa Bowl with Creamy Green Sauce

Cashews create a creamy base for this vegan take on green goddess dressing, which is flavored with herbs and apple cider vinegar. Drizzle it all over this bowl of quinoa and roasted vegetables for a wonderful vegan dinner or quick packable lunch that's done in 30 minutes.

Recipe Summary

Active: 25 minutes   **Total: 30 minutes**   **Servings: 4**

Nutrition Profile:

Heart Healthy	Egg Free	High Blood
Low-Calorie	Gluten-Free	Pressure
Dairy-Free	Vegetarian	Healthy Aging
Diabetes	Vegan	Healthy
Appropriate	Low Sodium	Immunity

Ingredients

4 cups broccoli florets
8 ounces cremini mushrooms (3 cups), quartered
2 large shallots, sliced
½ cup water
2 tablespoons extra-virgin olive oil, divided
½ teaspoon salt, divided
¼ cup fresh parsley leaves
¼ teaspoon ground pepper
¾ cup raw cashews
1 tablespoon cider vinegar
½ teaspoon reduced-sodium tamari or soy sauce

2 cups cooked quinoa
1 cup shredded red cabbage

Instructions

Step 1

Preheat oven to 425 degrees F.

Step 2

Put broccoli, mushrooms and shallots in a large bowl. Toss with 1 tablespoon oil, ¼ teaspoon salt, and ¼ teaspoon pepper to coat. Transfer to a large rimmed baking sheet and roast, tossing once, until the vegetables are soft and caramelized, about 20 minutes total.

Step 3

Meanwhile, in a blender, combine the cashews, water, parsley, vinegar, tamari (or soy sauce), and the remaining 1 tablespoon oil and ¼ teaspoon salt. Puree until smooth, stopping and scraping down the sides as needed.

Step 4

Divide the cooked quinoa, cabbage, roasted veggies, and sauce among four dishes.

Tips

Tip: People with celiac disease or gluten intolerance should use "gluten-free" soy sauces, as soy sauce might include wheat or other gluten-containing substances.

Nutritional Info

Per Serving:

341 Calories; Protein 12g; Carbohydrates 35.5g; Dietary Fiber 5.9g; Sugars 5g; Fat 18.5g; Saturated

Fat 2g; Vitamin A In 2755.6IU; Vitamin C 82mg; Folate 121mcg; Calcium 86mg; Iron 4.2mg; Magnesium

156mg; Potassium 889mg; Sodium 366mg

Day 21

Kale Salad with Beets & Wild Rice

A filling, colorful dinner salad made with beets and kale, chewy wild rice, and crunchy sunflower seeds. When the beets are sliced paper thin, they taste the best. If you have a mandolin or a vegetable slicer, use it.

Recipe Summary

Active: 20 minutes   **Total: 20 minutes**   **Servings: 4**

Nutrition Profile:

Heart Healthy	Egg Free	Nut-Free
Low-Calorie	Gluten-Free	Soy-Free
Dairy-Free	Vegetarian	Healthy
Diabetes	Vegan	Immunity
Appropriate	Low Sodium	

Ingredients

- 1 large bunch lacinato or curly kale, stems trimmed, chopped (8 cups)
- 1 cup cooked wild rice
- 1 medium beet, peeled, halved and very thinly sliced (2 ½ cups)
- 5 tablespoons Lemon-Tahini Dressing
- ⅓ cup toasted sunflower seeds

Instructions

Step 1

Combine beet, wild rice, kale and sunflower seeds in a large bowl. Include the dressing, toss until well coated. Serve within 1 - 2 hours.

Nutritional Info

Per Serving:
175 Calories; Protein 6g; Carbohydrates 16g; Dietary Fiber 4g; Sugars 3g; Fat 9g; Saturated Fat 1g; Vitamin A In 3233.1IU; Vitamin C 43mg; Folate 113mcg; Calcium 72.2mg; Iron 1.6mg; Magnesium 52mg; Potassium 403mg; Sodium 300mg

Day 22

Slow-Cooker Vegetarian Bolognese

This substantial vegetarian sauce uses beans instead of ground beef and is ready when you are, thanks to the crock pot. The preparation can be done quickly and easily in the morning before going to work. Dinner will be ready when you get home if you make some whole-wheat spaghetti to serve it over. If there are any leftovers, freeze them for a quick dinner later.

Recipe Summary

Active: 15 minutes	**Total: 4 hrs. 30 minutes**	**Servings: 8**

Nutrition Profile:

Heart Healthy	Low Sodium	Soy-Free
Low-Calorie	Nut-Free	Healthy Aging
Egg Free	High Blood	Healthy
Vegetarian	Pressure	Immunity

Ingredients

- 1 (28 ounce) can diced tomatoes, preferably San Marzano
- ½ cup dry white wine
- ½ cup low-sodium vegetable broth or water
- 3 tablespoons extra-virgin olive oil
- 2 tablespoons minced garlic
- ¼ teaspoon ground pepper
- 1 teaspoon Italian seasoning
- ½ teaspoon 1 cup chopped onion
- ½ cup chopped celery

- ½ cup chopped carrot
- salt
- 2 (15 ounce) cans no-salt-added cannellini beans or small white beans, rinsed
- ½ cup grated Parmesan cheese
- ¼ cup heavy cream
- 1 pound whole-wheat spaghetti
- ¼ cup chopped fresh basil

Instructions

Step 1

In a 5- to 6-quart slow cooker, mix together tomatoes, wine, broth (or water), onion, celery, carrot, oil, garlic, Italian seasoning, salt, and pepper. Cook for 4 hours on high or 8 hours on low. At the last minute of cooking, add the beans and cream. Keep warm.

Step 2

Meanwhile, bring a large saucepan of water to a boil. Cook spaghetti according to pack instructions; drain. Distribute the spaghetti among 8 bowls. Add the sauce, Parmesan, and basil on the top.

To prepare ahead of time: Sauce can be refrigerated for up to 4 days or frozen for up to 3 months (Step 1). When needed, thaw and reheat before serving.

Nutritional Info

Per Serving:

430 Calories;	63g; Dietary Fiber	Fat 3.5g;
Protein 15g;	6g; Sugars 6g; Fat	Cholesterol
Carbohydrates	12g; Saturated	12mg; Vitamin A

• • •

In 1999.3IU;
Vitamin C 14mg;
Folate 77.3mcg;
Calcium 146.9mg;

Iron 4mg;
Magnesium
143mg;
Potassium

762mg; Sodium
410mg

Day 24

Falafel Burgers

Pureed chickpeas, seasoned with the unique tastes of falafel, make superb veggie burgers. We cook the patties in two stages, browning them first in a skillet and then completing them in the oven. Tzatziki or tahini sauce, pickled red onions, lettuce, and tomatoes go on top of the burgers.

Recipe Summary

Active: 30 minutes   **Total: 1 hr.**   **Servings: 4**

Nutrition Profile:

Heart Healthy	Diabetes	Low Sodium
Low-Calorie	Appropriate	Nut-Free
High Fiber	Egg Free	Soy-Free
Dairy-Free	Vegetarian	Healthy Aging
	Vegan	

Ingredients

- ½ cup coarsely chopped onion
- 3 cloves garlic, crushed
- 1 medium jalapeño pepper, seeded and coarsely chopped
- ¾ cup fresh cilantro and/or parsley leaves
- 1 (15 ounce) can no-salt-added chickpeas, rinsed
- ¼ teaspoon baking soda
- 1 tablespoon extra-virgin olive oil

• • •

- 2 teaspoons ground cumin
- 1 teaspoon ground coriander
- ⅓ cup dry whole-wheat breadcrumbs or gluten-free breadcrumbs
- ¼ teaspoon salt
- 4 whole-wheat or gluten-free burger buns, split and toasted

Instructions

Step 1

In a food processor, pulse the onion, garlic, jalapeo, and cilantro (or parsley) until equally chopped. Insert chickpeas, cumin, coriander, baking soda and salt. Process until everything is nicely integrated.

Step 2

Transfer to a medium mixing bowl. Toss in the breadcrumbs. Refrigerate for 20 minutes after covering. (The breadcrumbs will be able to absorb any excess moisture this way.)

Step 3

Preheat the oven to 350 degrees F. Form the chickpea mixture into four 3-inch-diameter patties, using a generous 1/3 cup per patty.

Step 4

Heat the oil in a large skillet over medium heat. Cook the patties until brown and crispy on both sides, about 4 minutes per side. Carefully transfer the patties to a baking sheet and bake for 15 minutes, or until heated through and slightly puffed. Serve the patties on buns.

Nutritional Info

Per Serving:

261 Calories; Protein 10g; Carbohydrates 42g; Dietary Fiber 8g; Sugars 4g; Fat 7g; Saturated Fat

0.9g; Vitamin A In 225.7IU; Vitamin C 5mg; Folate 86mcg; Calcium 94mg; Iron 2.7mg;

Magnesium 68mg; Potassium 364mg; Sodium 505mg

Day 25

Easy Pea & Spinach Carbonara

Fresh pasta cooks faster than dried pasta, making it ideal for quick midweek dinners like this decadent but wholesome dish. The creamy sauce comes from eggs. They don't get thoroughly cooked, so choose pasteurized-in-the-shell eggs if you prefer.

Recipe Summary

Active: 20 minutes   Total: 20 minutes   Servings: 4

Nutrition Profile:

Heart Healthy
Low-Calorie
High Fiber
Diabetes
Appropriate
Vegetarian

Low Sodium
Nut-Free
High Calcium
Soy-Free
Bone Health
Healthy Aging

Healthy
Immunity
Low Added
Sugars

Ingredients

- 1 ½ tablespoons extra-virgin olive oil
- ½ cup panko breadcrumbs, preferably whole-wheat
- 1 small clove garlic, minced
- 3 large egg yolks
- 1 large egg
- ½ teaspoon 8 tablespoons grated Parmesan cheese, divided
- ¼ teaspoon salt
- 3 tablespoons finely chopped fresh parsley
- ground pepper
- 1 (9 ounce) package fresh tagliatelle or linguine
- 8 cups baby spinach
- 1 cup peas (fresh or frozen)

Instructions

Step 1

Place the 10 cups of water in a large pot, boil over high heat.

Step 2

Meanwhile, heat the oil in a large skillet over medium-high heat. Insert breadcrumbs and garlic; fry, stir occasionally, until toasted, about 2 minutes. Reallocate to a small bowl and stir in 2 tablespoons Parmesan and parsley. Set aside.

Step 3

In a medium mixing bowl, combine the remaining 6 tablespoons Parmesan, egg yolks, egg, pepper, and salt.

Step 4

Cook pasta for 1 minute in hot water, stirring occasionally. Cook for 1 minute more after adding the spinach and peas, or until the pasta is cooked. Reserve ¼ cup of the cooking water. Drain and transfer to a large mixing bowl.

Step 5

Slowly whisk the egg mixture with the saved cooking water. Add the mixture to the pasta in a slow, steady stream, stirring with tongs to incorporate. Serve with the remaining breadcrumb mixture on top.

Nutritional Info

Per Serving:

431 Calories; Protein 22g; Carbohydrates 51g; Dietary Fiber 8g; Sugars 2g; Fat 15g; Saturated Fat 3.9g; Cholesterol 223mg; Vitamin A In 8198IU; Vitamin C 55mg; Folate 53mcg; Calcium 246.1mg; Iron 6.1mg; Magnesium 96mg; Potassium 160mg; Sodium 584mg

Day 26

Hearty Tomato Soup with Beans & Greens

Garlicky kale and creamy white beans transform a simple canned tomato soup into a filling 10-minute lunch or dinner. For a heartier texture, use a soup with tomato bits. Look for a low- or reduced-sodium brand that has no more than 450 mg of sodium per serving.

Recipe Summary

Active: 10 minutes   **Total: 10 minutes**   **Servings: 4**

Nutrition Profile:

Heart Healthy	**Vegetarian**	**Healthy**
Low-Calorie	**Low Sodium**	**Immunity**
High Fiber	**Nut-Free**	**Healthy**
Diabetes	**High Calcium**	**Pregnancy**
Appropriate	**Soy-Free**	**Low Added**
Egg Free	**Bone Health**	**Sugars**
Gluten-Free	**Healthy Aging**	

Ingredients

- 2 (14 ounce) cans low-sodium hearty-style tomato soup
- 1 tablespoon olive oil
- 3 cups chopped kale
- ⅛ Teaspoon crushed red pepper (optional)
- 1 teaspoon minced garlic
- 1 (14 ounce) can no-salt-added cannellini beans, rinsed
- ¼ cup grated Parmesan cheese

Instructions

Step 1

Heat soup in a medium saucepan according to package instructions; simmer over low heat as you prepare the kale.

Step 2

Heat the oil in a large skillet over medium heat. Add the kale, cook, stirring, until wilted, about 1 - 2 minutes. Cook for 30 seconds after adding the garlic and crushed red pepper (if using). Stir the greens and beans into the soup and cook for 2 - 3 minutes, or until the beans are heated through.

Step 3

Pour the soup into four bowls. Serve with a sprinkling of Parmesan cheese on top.

Nutritional Info

Per Serving:

201 Calories;	Fat 1.4g;	Calcium 209.7mg;
Protein 6g;	Cholesterol	Iron 2mg;
Carbohydrates	3.6mg; Vitamin A	Magnesium
29g; Dietary Fiber	In 1637.1IU;	52mg; Potassium
5.9g; Sugars 1.1g;	Vitamin C 16.6mg;	257.4mg; Sodium
Fat 5g; Saturated	Folate 17mcg;	350.9mg

Day 27

Vegan Cauliflower Fettuccine Alfredo with Kale

Cooked cauliflower transforms into a thick, delicious sauce when mixed with melted cashews in this date-night-worthy vegan fettuccine Alfredo recipe. The creamiest results will come from a high-powered blender. To add fiber to this vegan pasta recipe, use whole-wheat fettuccine.

Recipe Summary

Active: 30 minutes	Total: 45 minutes	Servings: 6

• • •

Heart Healthy
Low-Calorie
Dairy-Free
Diabetes
Appropriate

Egg Free
Vegetarian
Vegan
Low Sodium
Soy-Free

Healthy Aging
Healthy
Immunity
Low Added
Sugars

Ingredients

- ½ cup fresh whole-wheat breadcrumbs, toasted
- 1 tablespoon chopped fresh parsley
- ½ teaspoon grated lemon zest
- 1 cup water
- 4 cups cauliflower florets (1 small head)
- 1 cup raw cashews
- 8 ounces whole-wheat fettuccine
- 4 cups lightly packed thinly sliced kale
- ¾ teaspoon salt
- 3 tablespoons lemon juice
- 2 tablespoons white miso
- 2 teaspoons garlic powder
- 2 teaspoons onion powder

Instructions

Step 1

Bring a big saucepan of water to a boil.

Step 2

In a small mixing dish, combine breadcrumbs, parsley, and lemon zest. Keep aside.

Step 3

Cook the cauliflower and cashews in the boiling water for 15 minutes, or until the cauliflower is extremely soft. Transfer the cauliflower and cashews to a blender using a slotted spoon.

Step 4

Cook, stirring periodically, for 10 minutes after adding the pasta to the boiling water. Add the kale and cook for another minute, or until the pasta is just soft. Return the pasta and kale to the saucepan after draining.

Step 5

In a blender, combine the lemon juice, miso, garlic powder, onion powder, salt, and 1 cup water; blend until smooth. Stir in the sauce until it is evenly distributed throughout the pasta. Serve with the breadcrumb mixture on top.

Nutritional Info

Per Serving:

325 Calories; Protein 13g; Carbohydrates 46.6g; Dietary Fiber 6.7g; Sugars 5.9g;	Fat 11g; Saturated Fat 1.9g; Vitamin A In 1119.1IU; Vitamin C 51.5mg; Folate 68.2mcg;	Calcium 72mg; Iron 3mg; Magnesium 89mg; Potassium 616mg; Sodium 522mg

Creamy Vegan Butternut Squash Carbonara

Carbonara, which is normally made with eggs, gets a vegan twist by using roasted and pureed butternut squash. In place of the cheese and bacon, a topping of ground almonds, garlic, and sage adds texture and herby, savory flavor.

Recipe Summary

Active: 45 minutes	**Total: 45 minutes**	**Servings: 8**

Nutrition Profile:

Heart Healthy	**Diabetes**	**Vegan**
Low-Calorie	**Appropriate**	**Low Sodium**
Dairy-Free	**Egg Free**	**Soy-Free**
	Vegetarian	

Ingredients

- 1 pound butternut squash, peeled, seeded and cut into 1-inch cubes (3 cups)
- 1 medium onion, chopped
- 4 garlic cloves, divided
- 1 teaspoon salt, divided
- 2 tablespoons tomato paste
- ½ cup almonds, coarsely ground
- 2 tablespoons extra-virgin olive oil, divided
- 1 tablespoon chopped fresh sage
- ¼ teaspoon ground pepper
- 1 pound whole-wheat spaghetti
- 1 cup "no-chicken" broth or vegetable broth, warmed
- 3 tablespoons nutritional yeast

• • •

Instructions

Step 1

Preheat oven to 400 degrees F. Boil a large pot of water for cooking spaghetti.

Step 2

In a large mixing bowl, combine the squash, onion, 2 garlic cloves, tomato paste, 1 tablespoon oil, and ¼ teaspoon salt and pepper. Spread the squash in an even layer on a large rimmed baking sheet and roast for 25 to 30 minutes, stirring once halfway through.

Step 3

Meanwhile, cook the pasta as directed on the package. Drain.

Step 4

The remaining 2 garlic cloves should be minced. Heat the remaining 1 tbsp. oil in a small skillet over medium heat. Add the almonds and garlic, minced. Cook, stirring regularly, for 3 minutes, or until the almonds are roasted and aromatic. Cook, stirring, for another minute after adding the sage and ¼ teaspoon salt. Set aside.

Step 5

Transfer the mixture to a blender once the squash is soft. Insert broth, nutritional yeast and the remaining ½ teaspoon salt. Puree until the mixture is completely smooth.

Step 6

Toss the spaghetti with the squash sauce and return to the pan. Add a heaping tbsp. of the almond mixture to each plate of pasta.

Nutritional Info

Per Serving:

147 Calories;	Saturated Fat	Iron 1.1mg;
Protein 4g;	0.4g; Vitamin A	Magnesium 26
Carbohydrates	In 2163.8IU;	mg; Potassium
21.2g; Dietary	Vitamin C 3.8mg;	154.2mg; Sodium
Fiber 2.5g; Sugars	Folate 72 mcg;	156.1mg
1.3g; Fat 3.8g;	Calcium 26mg;	

Day 29

Vegetable and Tofu Soup

Tofu has a reputation for being bland, but in this veggie-packed soup, it's anything but when marinated in Italian seasoning for up to four hours.

Recipe Summary

Active: 35 minutes	Total: 2 hrs. 35 minutes	Servings: 4

Nutrition Profile:

Heart Healthy	Dairy-Free	Egg Free
Low-Calorie	Diabetes	Gluten-Free
High Fiber	Appropriate	Vegetarian

• • •

Low Sodium   High Blood   Soy-Free
Nut-Free   Pressure   Healthy Aging

Ingredients

- 1 (12 ounce) package extra-firm, tub-style tofu (fresh bean curd), drained and cut into 3/4-inch cubes
- 2 tablespoons olive oil
- 2 cups reduced-sodium chicken broth
- 1 teaspoon dried Italian seasoning, crushed
- 3 cups sliced fresh button mushrooms (8 ounces)
- Nonstick cooking spray
- 1 (14.5 ounce) can no-salt-added diced tomatoes with basil, garlic and oregano, undrained
- ½ cup fresh or frozen peas, thawed
- ½ cup 1-inch pieces asparagus
- ½ cup chopped roasted red sweet pepper
- ¼ cup sliced green olives
- ⅓ cup oil-packed dried tomatoes, drained and finely chopped
- 1 pinch Shredded Parmesan cheese

Instructions

Step 1

Place tofu in a resealable plastic bag set in a small bowl. Pour in the oil and season with Italian seasoning. Close the bag and turn to coat the tofu. Refrigerate for 2 to 4 hours to marinate.

Step 2

Cook over medium-high heat in a 5- to 6-quart Dutch oven coated with cooking spray. Add unconfined tofu; cook 5 to 8 minutes or until tofu is browned, flipping once.

Step 3

Add broth and tomato paste. Bring the mixture to a boil. Reduce heat to low and add the mushrooms, peas, and asparagus. Cook for 5–7 minutes, or until vegetables are barely tender. Heat through the sweet pepper, dried tomatoes, and olives. Serve with cheese on top if desired.

Nutritional Info

Per Serving:
266 Calories; Protein 16g; Carbohydrates 19.2g; Dietary Fiber 9.8g; Sugars 10.7g; Fat 14g; Saturated Fat 1.8g; Vitamin A In 882.8IU; Vitamin C 34.6mg; Folate 50mcg; Calcium 182.8mg; Iron 3.3mg; Magnesium 68.1mg; Potassium 722.1mg; Sodium 474mg

Day 30

Salmon Salad

For a change of pace, consider a salmon salad instead of tuna salad. Olives, lemon, onion, and capers are added to this version.

Recipe Summary

Total: 10 minutes   Servings: 1

Nutrition Profile:

Low-Calorie

Low Carbohydrate	Dairy-Free Gluten-Free	Low Added Sugars

Ingredients

- ½ cup boneless, skinless canned salmon, flaked (2 ½ ounces)
- 1 tablespoon extra-virgin olive oil
- 1 teaspoon minced red onion, or to taste
- 1 tablespoon lemon juice
- 1 teaspoon rinsed and chopped capers
- 2 Kalamata olives, pitted and diced
- 1 teaspoon minced fresh parsley

Instructions

Step 1

Combine the salmon, oil, lemon juice, olives, red onion, parsley and capers in a medium bowl.

Tips

To prepare ahead of time: Refrigerate, covered up to 2 days.

Nutritional Info

Per Serving:

250 Calories;
Protein 13g;
Carbohydrates
3g; Dietary Fiber
0.3g; Sugars 0.6g;
Fat 21.7g;
Saturated Fat

3.3g; Cholesterol
45mg; Vitamin A
In 114.7IU;
Vitamin C 7.9mg;
Folate 6.2mcg;
Calcium 119.8mg;
Iron 0.6mg;

Magnesium
2.8mg; Potassium
28.6mg; Sodium
447mg

• • •

Day 30

Florentine Hash Skillet

To start your day, here's a super-quick all-in-one-skillet breakfast with hash browns, spinach, egg, and cheese.

Recipe Summary

Total: 10 minutes   **Servings: 1**

Nutrition Profile:

Low-Calorie	Vegetarian	Low Added
Low	High Calcium	Sugars
Carbohydrate	Bone Health	
Gluten-Free	Healthy Aging	

Ingredients

- ½ cup frozen hash browns or precooked shredded potatoes
- Pinch of freshly ground pepper
- ½ cup frozen chopped spinach
- Pinch of salt
- 1 teaspoon extra-virgin olive oil
- 1 large egg
- 2 tablespoons shredded sharp Cheddar cheese

Instructions

Step 1

Heat the oil in a small nonstick skillet over medium heat. In a pan, put hash browns and spinach. Break egg on top and sprinkle with salt, pepper and cheese.

Step 2

Cover, lower heat to medium and cook for 4 to 7 minutes, or until the hash browns begin to brown on the bottom, the egg is set, and the cheese is melted.

Tips

Shredded cooked potatoes can usually be found in the refrigerated produce or dairy sections of most supermarkets.

Nutritional Info

Per Serving:

225 Calories;
Protein 13.6g;
Carbohydrates
11g; Dietary Fiber
2.8g; Sugars 0.7g;
Fat 14.6g;

Saturated Fat 5g;
Cholesterol 200
mg; Vitamin A In
9557.5IU; Vitamin
C 9.2mg; Folate
140.3mcg;

Calcium 224.7mg;
Iron 2mg;
Magnesium 66mg;
Potassium
351.6mg; Sodium
371 mg